MOVE

Pamphlet Architecture was initiated in 1977 as an independent vehicle to criticize, question, and exchange views. Each issue is assembled by an individual author/architect. For more information, pamphlet proposals, or contributions please write to Pamphlet Architecture, c/o Princeton Architectural Press, 37 East 7th Street, New York, New York, 10003.

1	*Bridges*	S. Holl	1977*
2	*10 Californian Houses*	M. Mack	1978*
3	*Villa Prima Facie*	L. Lerup	1978*
4	*Stairwells*	L. Dimitriu	1979*
5	*The Alphabetical City*	S. Holl	1980
6	*Einstein Tomb*	L. Woods	1980*
7	*Bridge of Houses*	S. Holl	1981*
8	*Planetary Architecture*	Z. Hadid	1981*
9	*Rural and Urban House Types*	S. Holl	1983
10	*Metafisica Della Architettura*	A. Sartoris	1984*
11	*Hybrid Buildings*	J. Fenton	1985
12	*Building;Machines*	R. McCarter	1987
13	*Edge of a City*	S. Holl	1991
14	*Mosquitoes*	K. Kaplan/T. Krueger	1993
15	*War and Architecture*	L. Woods	1993
16	*Architecture as a Translation of Music*	E. Martin	1994
17	*Small Buildings*	M. Cadwell	1996
19	*Reading Drawing Building*	Michael Silver	1996
20	*Seven Partly Underground Rooms*	Mary-Ann Ray	1997
21	*Situation Normal...*	Lewis.Tsurumaki.Lewis	1998
22	*Other Plans: University of Chicago Studies*	Michael Sorkin Studio	2001

*   Out of print but available in the collection *Pamphlet Architecture 1–10*

pamphlet architecture #23

MOVE

SITES OF TRAUMA

JOHANNA SALEH DICKSON

PRINCETON ARCHITECTURAL PRESS / NEW YORK

Published by
Princeton Architectural Press
37 East Seventh Street
New York, New York 10003

For a free catalog of books, call 1.800.722.6657.
Visit our Web site at www.papress.com.

 This project is supported in part by an award from
the National Endowment for the Arts.

NATIONAL
ENDOWMENT
FOR THE ARTS

Editor: Nancy Eklund Later
Designer: Johanna Saleh Dickson

Special thanks to: Nettie Aljian, Ann Alter, Nicola Bednarek, Janet Behning, Megan Carey,
Penny Chu, Russell Fernandez, Clare Jacobson, Mark Lamster, Linda Lee, Nancy Levinson,
Katharine Myers, Jane Sheinman, Scott Tennent, Jennifer Thompson, and Deb Wood of
Princeton Architectural Press—Kevin C. Lippert, publisher

Library of Congress Cataloging–in–Publication Data

Dickson, Johanna Saleh, 1972–
   MOVE : sites of trauma / Johanna Saleh Dickson.
     p. cm.—(Pamphlet architecture ; no. 23)
   ISBN 1–56898–400–6 (alk. paper)
   1. Architecture—Human factors—Case studies. 2.
Architecture—Psychological aspects—Case studies. 3. MOVE
(Organization)—Case studies. 4. City
planning—Pennsylvania—Philadelphia—History—20th century. 5.
Post–traumatic stress disorder. I. Title. II. Series.
   NA2542.4 .D53 2002
   307.1'2'0974811—dc21
                                    2002012057

CONTENTS

THE MOVE CONFLICT   6

DESIGN WORK   Introduction   36

TRANSFORM / SUSTAIN   Johanna Saleh Dickson   38

PROSTHESIS   Mark Gardner   54
                             Henry S. Hsu
                             Brian Slocum

URBAN DENEWAL   Alexandra Schmidt-Ullrich   60
                             Thomas P. Kirchner

EVOLUTION OF TRAGEDY   Gaetane Michaux   66
                             Chris Warren
                             Richard McNamara

DPTNP   Todd Hoehn   72
                             Edowa Shimizu
                             Karen Tamir

CONTRIBUTORS   78

ACKNOWLEDGMENTS   79

CREDITS   80

"When dawn came again to west Philadelphia, it seemed that even the skies mourned. The blue skies of May 13 had given way to dark, low clouds. The late spring warmth of the day before had turned thick and oppressive. In the gray light of dawn, scattered firefighters stood among the ruins, playing water across still smoldering debris. Amid the rising steam and smoke, crumbling structures emerged from the darkness—the fire walls that had once separated the homes on this street. They were the

THE MOVE CONFLICT On May 13, 1985, a bomb was dropped on a rowhouse in west Philadelphia. The bomb was an attempt to forcibly evict the residents of 6221 Osage Avenue, the home of a radical organization called MOVE. The explosionignited a can of gasoline on the roof of the home, causing the roof to burn. The fire burned freely for four hours before any effort was made to extinguish it. In the end, eleven MOVE members were killed (including five children), sixty-one homes were destroyed, one hundred homes were wrecked, and two hundred and fifty people were left homeless.

The MOVE organization was founded in the early 1970s by a man who called himself John Africa. Members adopted a "back-to-nature" lifestyle and actively protested what they considered to be the "profanities" of modern society: the destruction of nature, racism, and oppression. By 1985, MOVE's protests against the city of Philadelphia had intensified into a volatile, aggressive conflict.

The story of what happened on May 13 is a complicated and confused one. The night before, the residents of the 6200 block of Pine, Osage, and Addison avenues were evacuated. Trusting that they would be able return home by the following evening, as they had been promised, few residents took any personal property with them; many even left their pets at home. The next morning, MOVE refused to evacuate the house when asked to, so city officials went to extreme measures to force them out. The police fired thousands of rounds of ammunition at the house and later attempted to enter it through the adjacent rowhouse by blowing a hole in the shared party wall. The members of MOVE remained inside.

It was reported that the intention of the bomb was to blow a small hole in the roof into which teargas could be inserted. This is somewhat questionable, considering that the bomb was said to be constructed with the powerful C-4 explosive, obtained illegally by the Philadelphia Police Department from the FBI in preparation for the attack.[1] After the bomb's explosion, the city's police and fire departments decided to let the resulting fire burn as a means of dismantling the large steel-reinforced bunker that MOVE had built on their roof. But long after the bunker was destroyed the fire continued to burn freely. People all across the city watched on live television as the fire burned through three blocks of rowhouses. Mayor Wilson Goode, Philadelphia's first black mayor, watched from a television in his office: what he saw looked like war.[2]

The MOVE bombing was one of the most tragic events in Philadelphia's long history, a tragedy that was only intensified by the city's response. Within days of the bombing, the city tried to bury the event and its physical remains as quickly as possible. Officials made an unrealistic promise to have the residents back in their homes by Christmas, only seven months later. This left no time to stop and think about what would be the best way to rebuild, both psychologically and physically, after such a disaster. The party walls, which remained largely intact after the blaze, were leveled and reconstruction began almost immediately. The new construction that went up in the subsequent months was so shoddy that residents' roofs leaked with the first rainfall. The contractor responsible for the construction would later go to jail for embezzling more than $100,000 in recovery funds.

Boarded-up rowhouses on Osage Avenue today

In the new homes, the front porch was replaced with a single step and a steel gate, which, aside from being unattractive and uncharacteristic of the vernacular architecture of the city, also served to further isolate the residents from their community by removing a space so essential for communication. The house at 6221 Osage was rebuilt like the others, but its only occupant has been the Philadelphia Police Department. Since its 1986 reconstruction, the house has been monitored twenty-four hours a day by police officers to prevent an unlikely reoccupation by MOVE.

No criminal charges were ever filed against the city officials who made the ultimately tragic decisions, but the city paid millions in civil fines to the remaining MOVE members as compensation for the loss of their children. Despite reconstruction and financial settlements, the loss of lives and homes has never been justly acknowledged.

The impact of this event was far-reaching. Beyond MOVE and the small neighborhood that was directly affected, the tragedy affected everyone who lived in Philadelphia at the time. The organizations in the city that participated in and aggravated the conflict with MOVE were many, from almost every level of its hierarchy: the Mayor's office (encompassing three administrations), the court system (at all levels, including the Supreme Court), and the police force, as well as community organizations, negotiators, neighbors, the media, and, of course, the MOVE members

The aftermath on Osage Avenue

themselves. Everyone involved operated within a given belief system, employing their own discourses as a means of communication, aggression, and self-defense.

News of the tragedy spread across the country: some saw it as an accident; others saw the circum-stances of the tragedy as particular to black urban communities. Seventeen years later, the city of Philadelphia is now attempting to buy out the residents of the destroyed blocks from their rebuilt homes so that they can level the site once again and put an end to the heavy muni-cipal costs that the constant main-tenance of the

"If a person is born in a building, and is never shown the outside, the building is all that they know, and when a fire breaks out, the person will run all over in seek of relief, from the basement to the attic, for this is the extent of their comprehension."

homes requires. At the time of this writing, a number of residents are refusing to be bought out and continue to live in their homes, surrounded by the boarded-up homes of their former neighbors. "There has been no recovery," said Reverend Mary Laney, a spiritual leader in Philadelphia, "It doesn't feel like there has been any real redemption out of it. You can get through horrible things and painful times, but there's usually something that has been brought out of it that redeems it. I don't think people have any sense of that."[3]

TRANSFORMATION Examination of the MOVE conflict through the perspective of Post-Traumatic Stress Disorder (PTSD) provides a framework for developing a method of recovery that is both psychological and architectural in nature. If a connection to this place of home and community can be regained through architectural transformations, perhaps it can promote similar internal transformations in the individuals affected by this conflict. An appropriate architectural response to this tragedy is sought by looking at the history of the MOVE conflict and the issues that define it. Before addressing the specific events, however, a psychological foundation upon which to support the analysis must be constructed.

A traumatic event can have particular conditions, both in its occurrence and its aftermath, that act to impede its resolution. PTSD is defined clinically by the American Psychiatric Association as "the development of characteristic symptoms following a psychologically distressing event that is outside the range of usual human experience," the most significant symptoms being the "reexperiencing [of] the traumatic event, and numbing of general responsiveness." The types of traumatic events that can lead to PTSD include "serious threat to one's life or physical integrity; serious threat or harm to one's children, spouse, or other close relatives and friends; sudden destruction of one's home or community."[4] The individual feels untrusting and disconnected from the people and places that surround him (his present), because his mind is trapped in the context of the trauma. Reexperience of the trauma "permits the past (memory) to relive itself in the present, in the form of intrusive images and thoughts."[5] Recovery after trauma is only possible once the experience has been properly constructed as a memory, allowing the individual affected to move forward while still living with and learning from his traumatic experience. If a resting place for the traumatic memory cannot be found, the onset of PTSD is likely.

The conditions of the soldiers of the Vietnam War, both in Vietnam and in the United States when they returned home, led to thousands of cases of PTSD among veterans. In fact, it was the overwhelming number of cases of veterans returning from Vietnam with serious psychological problems that led the psychiatric community to officially accept the diagnosis of PTSD in 1980. An army is a social construction like any community; it is established on a foundation of shared expectations and values. In Vietnam, the causes that the soldiers were fighting for were unclear, from the larger moral (political) issues to more specific ones, like the killing of civilians. The oppressive physical and social conditions left soldiers feeling that they could not trust anyone outside their own company.

Once discharged, the soldiers were sent back to the U.S. alone—not with their company, as was the policy in previous wars—often arriving home less than two days after leaving the battlefield. In World War II, soldiers returned home with their entire company. The voyage took months, which—consciously or not—allowed for some sort of shared processing of the trauma they had experienced. The WWII veterans also returned home as heroes. For the veterans of the Vietnam War, the climate in the U.S. was less than supportive. With no outlet for communalization of their traumatic memory, many veterans turned inward and have never recovered. In *The Harmony of Illusions: Inventing Post-Traumatic Stress Disorder*, author Allan Young examined the historic and anthropological significance of the disorder. "The psychological pathology of the individual, the microcosmos," he maintained, "has a mirror image in the moral pathology of the collectivity, the social macrocosmos. The collective secret is a willful ignorance of traumatic acts and a denial of post-traumatic suffering."[6]

Proper processing of the traumatic memory is inextricably linked to the individual's larger social context. Jonathan Shay, a noted psychologist and researcher of PTSD, maintains, "Healing from trauma depends on communalization of the trauma—being able safely to tell the story to someone who is listening and who can be trusted to retell it truthfully to others in the community."[7] Thus, the traumatic event might occur at the level of the individual, even if there are many individuals involved, but the outcome, whether it is recovery or the onset of PTSD, is determined at a communal level. Transformation is a primary concept in PTSD. The trauma and its aftermath have elicited a negative transformation in the individual, through the onset of the disorder and the incapacitating symptoms that accompany it. Shay asserts, "Unhealed combat trauma—and unhealed severe trauma from any source—destroys the unnoticed substructure of democracy, the cognitive and social capabilities that enable a group of people to freely construct a narrative of their own future."[8] Recovery is equally dependent upon transformation: a positive transformation achieved by the reprocessing and communalization of the event. This transformation allows for growth and insight, focusing the present on the future rather than the past.

Most of the work written about the MOVE conflict has made comparisons between what occurred on the 6200 block of Osage Avenue and what occurs in war—in particular, the Vietnam War. Conflicting images of morality represented by aggressive MOVE members, innocent MOVE children, aggressive police officers, and innocent neighbors illustrate that "the same lack of moral conviction that haunted the Vietnam War echoes through the Vietnam redux on Osage Avenue."[9] At least six of the police officers involved in the MOVE bombing had served in Vietnam.[10] As for the MOVE members themselves, their leader was a war veteran, and the younger members, like most people of their generation, were strongly affected by the war. Kathleen Neal Cleaver, lawyer and civil rights activist, maintained:

> The adults in MOVE had bought into the glorification of violence that suffused our society during the Vietnam War era. They were survivors and observers of the war psychosis that Vietnam brought

to a boil in black ghettoes already seething with drug abuse, crime, and family deterioration. At the same time, the police in the neighborhood were recipients of the transfer of military tactics from Vietnam into domestic police action. These men in uniform, above all, brought the war home.[11]

The post-traumatic environment that has surrounded the MOVE conflict has not permitted the communalization necessary to initiate recovery, which is clear seventeen years later as the city of Philadelphia tries again to demolish this community and erase the memory of what happened there. Memory, at both the individual and collective levels, is connected as much to the present as to the past. According to anthropologist and PTSD researcher Allan Young, collective memory, so crucial in the communalization process, "can reside not only in individual minds but in practices, standards, apparatuses, and social relations."[12] Architecture can act as a vehicle for this collective memory. Psychologically, architecture can serve as a representation of history and of people's needs and desires. Physically, architecture can create an environment in which the communalization process can take place and a collective memory can be established. For the victims of the MOVE conflict, the past and the present must be resolved before a future can be constructed. Reconstruction of the traumatic memory through architecture can free the present from the past. However, any act of transformation must recognize recovery as a process of construction, just as the trauma was a process of destruction.

"Warfare is not an event, but a process... traumatization is repetitive, often continuous for long periods of time."

The MOVE conflict did not occur in isolation, rather it was an intensification of tensions that existed, and still exist, in distressed urban areas throughout the country, particularly in black communities. Philadelphia is infamous for the brutality against blacks that its police force has inflicted, and much of MOVE's protest and self-defense was a reaction to such injustices. It is reasonable to question whether the city would have allowed sixty-one homes to burn to the ground if the conflict had taken place in a white neighborhood. By 1985, however, the war that MOVE was trying to fight was no longer justified; their actions had become antagonistic and confused. In the end, neither the city nor MOVE acted justly, and the only innocent victims were the neighbors. It is the lack of moral clarity in a conflict that involves so many significant issues that has made the MOVE conflict so difficult to resolve.

MOVE

Vincent Leaphart, the future leader of MOVE, was born on July 26, 1931, in Mantua, a neighborhood just north of Powelton Village in west Philadelphia. His experiences in childhood and early adulthood were significant but by no means extraordinary. His mother died when he was young, and he placed the blame for her death on the hospital that treated her. In his late teens, combat experience as a foot soldier in the Korean War heightened the resentment he already felt toward the "system" of American society.

Although basically illiterate, Leaphart became known for making observations and formulating ideas about the workings of society. In the early 1970s, he began calling himself John Africa. He took the name Africa not just because he was an African-American but also because he saw Africa as the source of all life. He met a young social worker from the University of Pennsylvania, a white man named Donald Glassey, who became fascinated by his ideas and offered to write them down. Together they created a three-hundred page manuscript known as "The Guidelines." These writings became the bible of John Africa's organization, originally referred to as the "Christian Movement for Life," then "The Movement," and later, simply MOVE.

Inspired by John Africa's words, and often in desperate search of "answers," MOVE members attracted numerous followers to their organization, both black and white. Many of them had grown up in the city, had succumbed to drugs and violence, and felt similar frustrations with American society and their place in it. MOVE members tried to connect with nature's way of life by eating only

"We believe in natural law, the government of self."

raw food, using no soap or electricity, and practicing no form of birth control. All members adopted the surname Africa and believed, unquestioningly, in the words of their leader. According to John Africa, the trauma of modern society was in the experience of everyday life, in the experience of war, drugs, murder, and poverty. Recovery from this trauma demanded revolution. A flyer from the early 1970s promoting the organization insisted, "Revolution means total change, a complete dissociation from everything that is causing the problems you are revolting against."[13] For MOVE, dissociation was not achieved by relocating to a more "natural" place. Members believed in an urban revolution, one that could happen in the city of Philadelphia through the will of its citizens. MOVE envisioned a city returned to its natural state, an undoing of all the traumas and negative transformations that had brought it to its current condition. Michael Boyette, author of *"Let it Burn"*: *The Philadelphia Tragedy*, observed:

> Perhaps they could see the forests rising again from beneath the asphalt of the cities, the cars rusting and returning to the earth, the skyscrapers crumbling into piles of stone, and the choked and polluted creeks of what was now west Philadelphia running clear under canopies of virgin green. That was the vision that had brought them here.[14]

In 1974, MOVE settled into a house at 309 North 33rd Street in Powelton Village, a diverse, liberal neighborhood in west Philadelphia. MOVE's presence in the neighborhood was not a problem until their

"John Africa wanted to tear up the black-top and let food grow everywhere."

Activity in front of MOVE house, Powelton Village

practice of composting garbage in their backyard led to an increase in the number of rats and cockroaches in the area. Neighbors complained directly to MOVE members but were met with angry threats. Tensions increased as some residents filed complaints against MOVE with the city. MOVE built a wooden platform in front of their house from which members preached their philosophy to onlookers. They spoke through bullhorns and sold T-shirts; people were invited to approach and listen. MOVE was unapologetic in its efforts to spread the word and took little or no heed of neighbors' complaints.

"It's not MOVE that threatens or intimidates anybody, the government does that."

Nonviolence was a defining feature of the MOVE organization in its early years; member's protests were aggressive only in the extreme nature of their beliefs and their obsessive adherence to them. At the time, the city of Philadelphia was under the leadership of Frank Rizzo, a former police officer turned mayor who made no apologies for police brutality.

Armed MOVE members, May 20, 1977

One MOVE member was drawn to the organization after her brother was arrested for a traffic violation and was found hung in his jail cell a few hours later. Most interactions between MOVE and the police ended violently. As MOVE wrote in its self-published book 25 Years on the MOVE, "If they came with guns we'd use guns too. We don't believe in death-dealing guns, we believe in life. But the cops wouldn't be so quick to attack us if they had to face the same stuff they dished out so casually on unarmed defenseless folk."[15] A fourteen-month standoff between MOVE and the city of Philadelphia began on May 20, 1977, the first time MOVE members appeared on their stagelike porch wearing military-style clothing and wielding weapons. By standing in front of their house with rifles, MOVE declared its intention to defend itself.

By this time MOVE members had long ceased paying their utility bills and had refused city inspectors admission to the house, reportedly threatening to kill themselves and their children if inspectors ventured inside. After numerous attempts to evict MOVE from their home had failed, the courts granted permission for a blockade and subsequently shut off gas lines and water mains to the house. A settlement was proposed by city negotiators that would have released all incarcerated MOVE members from jail if the organization promised to vacate the house. But this soon fell apart when MOVE made it clear that it would only relocate elsewhere in Philadelphia.

City officials visit MOVE house during standoff

The fact that such a bargain was ever suggested indicates the power that MOVE had over the city, a power fueled by fear of the unknown. Very few people talked directly to members of MOVE or knew what went on inside their house. A number of citizens tried to act as mediators between MOVE and the city in hopes of preventing a seemingly inevitable outbreak of violence, but because MOVE placed no trust in anything promised to it by the city, the organization was unwilling to negotiate.

"MOVE juxtaposed so many goals that the resulting mixture became unstable and essentially contradictory."

The conflict in Powelton Village finally came to an end on August 8, 1978, when the standoff escalated into violence. Shots were fired, presumably from inside the MOVE compound, resulting in an exchange of gunfire, the unnecessary death of a Philadelphia police officer, the severe beating of a MOVE member, and the demolition of the organization's house. The three police who brutally beat an unarmed MOVE member as he emerged from the house were acquitted without a trial, despite the fact that the beating was caught on videotape. Nine MOVE members were convicted and given sentences ranging from thirty to one hundred years each for the death of the police officer.

Violence erupts between MOVE and the city of Philadelphia, August 8, 1979

The MOVE organization reestablished its headquarters on Osage Avenue, in the quiet working-class west Philadelphia neighborhood of Cobbs Creek. By the 1960s, Cobbs Creek was the largest neighborhood of black home-owners in the city. With a history plagued by forced and voluntary migration, a black home-owning neighborhood was not terribly common at the time and indicated a desire to establish a firm connection to place. When MOVE arrived on Osage Avenue, many of its new neighbors sympathized with members, having seen the injustices that had occurred in Powelton Village, and accepted them into their

community. It soon became clear, however, that MOVE's lifestyle would create the same problems in Cobbs Creek that it had in Powelton Village. MOVE's presence on Osage Avenue would ultimately sever the connection between the neighbors and their place of home and community.

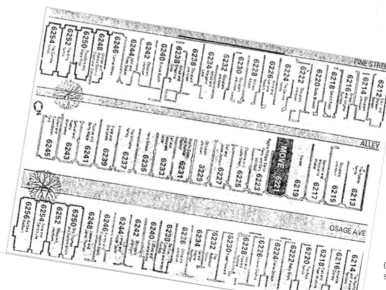

Cobbs Creek, location of the second MOVE house

19

MODIFICATION

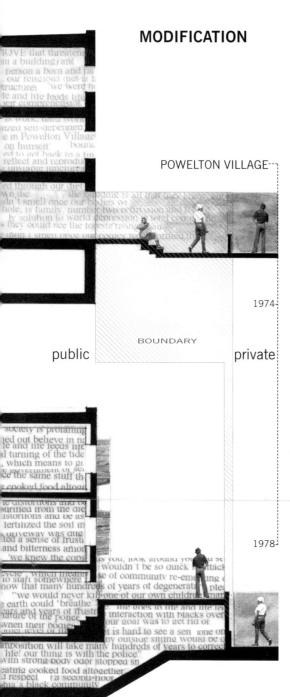

POWELTON VILLAGE

1974

BOUNDARY

public   private

1978

"Imagine the social world as a physical space, then imagine a map of the space representing a soldier's sense of social connectedness."[16] According to Jonathan Shay, once the capacity for social trust is destroyed as a result of trauma—an individual's map is diminished in scope. Many individuals were drawn to MOVE because their past experiences had already initiated a process of social disconnection; their maps had already begun to change. Most members of MOVE would eventually become completely disconnected from their larger community, their families and neighbors, their city and country. As the conflict with their community escalated, their social world became limited to the physical space of a fifteen-foot-wide Philadelphia rowhouse. This was the only space they had control of, so they sought to appropriate it through modification. One of the most fascinating aspects of the MOVE conflict is that it was marked by a concrete, physical spatiality.

MOVE's increasing isolation from its community was manifest in the way it transformed the exterior of its houses. In Powelton Village, a wooden stage was constructed on top of the porch. This six-foot-high platform extended from the front of the house to an eight-foot fence at the edge of the property. The front porch, or stoop, so characteristic of Philadelphia rowhouse architecture, acts as a communication space that occupies the boundary between outside and inside, between public and private. MOVE's first modification of this boundary space was intended to create a space that mediated between their home and the city, a space that allowed for communication while providing self-defense through physical separation.

MOVE lived in the house on Osage Avenue for five years before making any modifications to its exterior. The organization's members clearly wanted to become part of a larger community, but their radical lifestyle and cultlike obedience to the words of John Africa (who had allegedly become extremely paranoid, possibly due to schizophrenia) would eventually destroy any fragile ties that members had to their new community. By 1983, the transformations to 6221 Osage Avenue had begun, and this time the aim appeared to be complete fortification, seclusion, and defense. The front of the house was boarded up, and residents began to use the back entrance of the house exclusively, transforming the front porch into a void. Through the skylight in the second-floor bathroom, materials were piled onto the roof that were then used to construct two small rectangular structures fortified with steel sheeting. Small holes were cut into their sides. One of MOVE's neighbors observed, "There was no mistaking what they were. They were fortified bunkers. And the holes were gun ports."[17] Neighbors had been watching for months as MOVE members hauled barrels of dirt out of their house. After the bombing it would be revealed that a log cabin–like structure had been built under the front porch. Like the bunker, it was reinforced with steel and designed so that its occupants could shoot from inside.

The notion of dwelling as a modification of one's environment, the act of leaving a trace, is addressed by scholar Ivan Illich in his book *H²O and the Waters of Forgetfulness*. There he refers to space as "stuff, seen through Western eyes as an expanse, rather than a

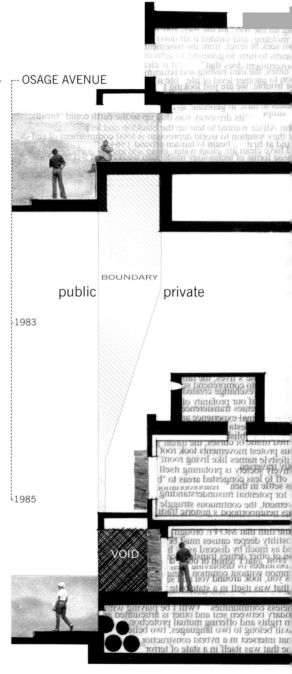

OSAGE AVENUE

BOUNDARY

public   private

1983

1985

VOID

receptacle that can be occupied and modified."[18] According to Illich, dwelling as a form of imprinting life on urban space has virtually disappeared from most modern cities. MOVE used its house as a receptacle, seeking to modify it as a means of appropriation, to strengthen the bond to home as the bond to community collapsed.

As MOVE members spent more and more time secluded within the confines of their rowhouse, their only way of connecting with nature was through their immediate physical space: the interior of their house, the roof, the backyard, and the basement. As they built up the exterior of the house, the interior was stripped down. They burned and

The MOVE house at 6221 Osage Ave., c. 1984, boarded up, bunker and bullhorn in place

scraped the paint from the walls. All of the wood surfaces were stripped down to the bare wood. Each day they scrubbed all the interior surfaces clean with water. The rooms were stripped of identity; they had no furniture and were never referred to by names such as "living room" or "bedroom." Outside, MOVE "dug up the driveway so the earth could breathe."[19] They used their basement, roof, and backyard as extensions of their interior living space.

It was MOVE's methods of occupation and modification of its environment that ultimately brought members into direct conflict with their neighbors and the city. Illich maintained that "the post-industrialist city is one of homogenous, indiscrete space where an individual feels compelled to live in a space without qualities and expects everyone else to stay within the bounds of his or her own skin."[20] The members of MOVE did not stay within the bounds of their own skin, nor within the bounds of their own backyard. Smell was the first thing to cross the boundary between MOVE and its neighbors. The smell of composting vegetable matter and human feces was intolerable to the neighbors. Eventually the rats and cockroaches that accompanied MOVE's back-to-nature lifestyle began to infest neighbors' homes as well. MOVE also installed bullhorns on their house from which they preached their ideology and demanded the release of imprisoned members. This was done with the deliberate use of excessive profanity, day and night. Even the view of MOVE's bunker from their homes

"If our profanity offends you, look around you and see how destructively society is profaning itself."

violated the neighbors' privacy by weakening their sense of security. Both intentionally (with the bullhorn and bunker) and unintentionally (with smells and vermin), MOVE invaded its neighbors' homes. It was these severe disruptions of privacy that began to sever the connection between MOVE and its neighbors, and between the neighbors and their own homes. MOVE's lifestyle could not be contained within the confined space of a rowhouse, so it transgressed

"There was no sleep and every other word was motherfucker."

the boundaries between outside and inside, between public and private.

The city of Philadelphia had numerous violations committed by MOVE on file that could have been considered grounds for eviction, but city officials feared the radical group and, although the situation was clearly volatile, did nothing. Neighbors felt helpless as they watched MOVE members walk from rooftop to rooftop armed with rifles. By April 1985, after living with MOVE for more than six years, the neighbors' frustrations had turned to fear. Clifford Bond, a longtime Osage Avenue resident, acted as a spokesperson for his fellow neighbors when they went before the governor of Pennsylvania on April 30, 1985. "We are here to let the governor know about the disquietude and general state of terror we are forced to live under by the MOVE organization."[21] They made a public appeal for help to the Republican governor, thus forcing the Democratic mayor to take immediate action. On May 13, the city responded.

" We were hostages in our own house."

The MOVE conflict was about transformations, both literal and metaphorical. It was about the transformation of an ordinary man named Vincent Leaphart into a radical prophet named John Africa; the transformation of his followers and their way of viewing the world, of reacting to it, and living in it; the transformation of the organization's home into a compound

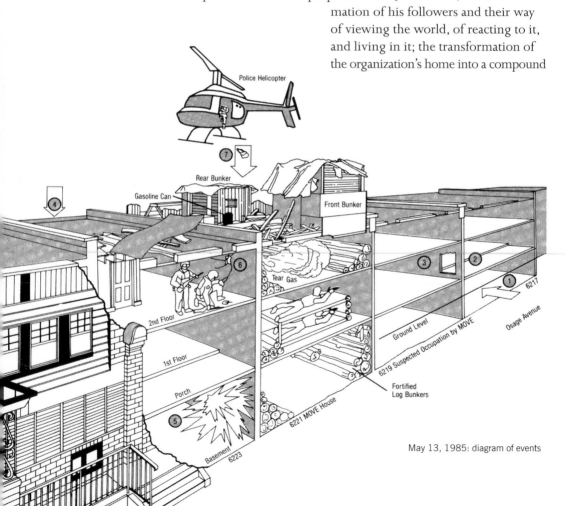

May 13, 1985: diagram of events

Facade and porch fragments that withstood the fire and would soon be leveled

and a bunker; and of its occupants into warriors. It was about the transformation of a community into helpless victims and the transformation of a neighborhood into a pile of rubble. Each of these transformations represents the MOVE conflict as the war that it was and the process that built it. As sociologist Robin Wagner-Pacifici noted, "It is the story of a house that underwent a strange transformation....It was a house that was itself in a state of terror."[22] It was a process that began in 1971 and erupted fourteen years later, and it is a process that continues for many of those affected by the trauma. It is also a process not limited to the specific context in which the MOVE conflict occurred.

RELATION

There are numerous examples of traumatic events from which there has been no recovery, where inappropriate responses in an event's aftermath have lead to PTSD at a communal level. One such example occurred on February 26, 1972, in Buffalo Creek, West Virginia. A dam holding 132 million gallons of coal slag and water broke, creating a twenty-foot wall of water that quickly flooded the hollow below, where many small villages were located. Within less than an hour, 125 people were dead, and 4,000 of Buffalo Creek's 5,000 inhabitants were homeless. Pittston Coal, the mining company that employed most of the people in the area, maintained the dam and was aware of its instability. The company refused to claim any responsibility for the disaster.

The survivors of the Buffalo Creek flood were traumatized. They saw loved ones killed, they saw neighbors' dead bodies wash past them, and they saw their homes ripped to pieces. A few of the homes were cleaned up, but as one resident observed, "A smell still hung in the air for more than a year later and the warped boards continued to emit streaks of oily black mud from the deposits that had caked under the floors and between the walls."[23] Many of the destroyed homes had been company-issued cabins that residents had modified over the years. Kai Erikson, a sociologist who studied the effects of the Buffalo Creek flood on the community, noted that "a home that has grown along with one, literally been built around one, is not simply an expression of one's taste; it is the outer edge of one's personality, a part of the self itself. And the loss of that part of the self, as researchers have noted in other disaster situations, is akin to the loss of flesh."[24]

The victims of the flood were further traumatized by events that took place after the flood. Homes declared in precarious condition were marked with a giant X and bulldozed, with no consent from the home-owners. HUD established trailer camps for the homeless in an area outside Buffalo Creek but made no effort to place people in proximity to their former neighbors. For the residents of Buffalo Creek, community did not mean the entire hollow population of 5,000, but the families that lived in the few houses located near theirs. So although everyone at the HUD camps had experienced similar traumas, people felt completely isolated.

In addition, the structure of the trailer camps did not promote the establishment of new communities. There were no open spaces and no front porches that, as Erikson noted, would "act as a zone of transition between the privacy of the inside world and the communality of the outside world. In most of Appalachia, where life is centered on the front stoop, one's door forms a sensitive boundary between the interior and the exterior."[25] Within a week of the flood the railroads were repaired and the mines were back in operation, but many families were forced to live in the trailers for more than two years. By 1975, only 100 homes had been rebuilt while $27 million in flood emergency funds was used to build a highway through Buffalo Creek.

Some 615 survivors were given psychiatric examinations a year and half after the flood in connection wtih a class-action lawsuit filed against Pittson Coal. And although this incident occurred before PTSD was officially established as a psychological diagnosis, the study indicated that 93 percent of those examined had developed an "identifiable emotional disorder."[26] The symptoms were the same as those seen in PTSD: disconnectedness, lack of trust, reexperience of the trauma. Every victim felt like they were experiencing these symptoms alone. The Buffalo Creek flood affected the entire community, but it was the post-traumatic events that destroyed it. And there was no larger community to which the victims could turn; their government took advantage of the razing of the ground that the flood had performed by building a new highway in Buffalo Creek. The victims of the flood had no opportunity for communalization; a collective memory of the event was never established.

Adaptation and recovery in a post-traumatic situation is critically dependent upon the development of a strong "trauma membrane," defined as a protective mebrane of support on social, economic, and personal levels.[27] Such support can make it possible for the victims not simply to adjust after a traumatic experience but to transcend the experience through transformation. It is possible for a traumatic experience to have an ultimately positive outcome. This was the case in the Great Chicago Fire of 1871. "It's black, bleak desolation, its skeleton streets, its shapeless masses of brick and mortar, its gaunt and jagged spires, only remnants of walls but yesterday so proud and stately, stared at me from every point," one of Chicago's citizens wrote on October 9,

Destruction in Buffalo Creek, West Virginia

1871.[28] The night before, a massive fire claimed the lives of 300 people, destroyed 17,500 homes, and left 100,000 people homeless. A full one-third of the city's structure was wiped out. The fire was at a scale that affected the entire community of Chicago, much in the way that the Buffalo Creek flood affected that entire community, albeit smaller. The Great Fire was a traumatic event for those who experienced it, but the post-traumatic atmosphere in the city was one that allowed people to come together and rebuild their city. The process of communalization, in this case, happened at a national scale, as survivors were asked to share their stories with people from different places. "They told and retold their stories because the fire was the most remarkable thing that had ever happened to them, and because talking about it was a way to try to capture its terror and significance through memory."[29]

The Great Chicago Fire is unlike the traumas that were experienced in the MOVE conflict or the Buffalo Creek flood; the scale was far greater, and the catastrophe was not an act of willful negligence. The more important distinction, however, is that in Chicago there was not a deeper process of traumatization that continued after the event itself, which made it possible for the Great Chicago Fire to become a great example of the potential for recovery that exists in a trauma of place. Donald Miller, historian and author of *City of the Century*, wrote that "the fire was a fresh beginning, almost an opportunity."[30] He described how after the fire the atmosphere in the city was optimistic and so "conducive to experiment and improvisation"[31] that the city literally reinvented itself and the industries that it contained. The Pullman railway car, the refrigerator car, and the modern packing plant were all conceived of in Chicago shortly after 1871.

The potential for new architecture was so great in Chicago that a number of young architects moved there after the fire just to take part in its rebuilding. Many of the burned districts were quickly rebuilt as they had been before, but the spirit of transformation was strong and many architects applied new materials and methods of construction that would revolutionize modern architecture. Miller noted, "Chicago's first skyscraper architects had a strong regional consciousness and the sense that they were making history in a part of America only recently claimed from the wilderness."[32] The term Chicago Construction refers to the basic steel skeletal system that created the structure for the modern skyscraper, and new laws regarding fireproofing in construction ensured that these buildings were safe. John Wellborn Root, a writer and architect, wrote in

Photograph of Chicago shortly after the Great Fire

1890 about Chicago and the West. He observed that there was no time for art in the initial building of Chicago, then described the intense transformation that occurred after the fire. It was a "long time full of deadness, except of physical force, then a sudden bursting of art into exuberant flower."[33]

MEMORY

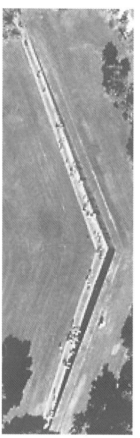

Aerial image of the Vietnam Veterans Memorial

For the veterans of the Vietnam War, the communalization process could not occur in the place of trauma; a new context for a collective memory was created in Washington, D.C., at the Vietnam Veterans Memorial. Designed by architect Maya Lin, the memorial is remarkably illustrative of the need for survivors of a traumatic event to have a way to respond to what they have experienced. Barely visible on approach, the memorial consists of a V-shaped wall wedged into the landscape like a book opened wide. The wall creates a passageway, submerged at its center to a depth of ten feet. The recognition of war as a loss of individual lives is achieved at the memorial through the inscription of the name of every person who died in the Vietnam War on the black granite wall. The omission of figures on the wall acknowledges that a few faces should not be chosen to represent thousands of individuals, and the highly polished black granite surface lets the visitors' own reflection become a brief representation of a life that has been lost. The Vietnam Veterans Memorial is not an idealized commemoration of war; it is not about heroes and glory, it is about death and loss. Yet there is a subliminal sense of rebirth and immortality, achieved through the simulated process of burial and reemergence that defines passage along the wall. It is about accepting the loss and moving forward.

Although the memorial is nonreactive in that its form is fixed, there is something subconscious in the power of its design that creates in visitors a desire to react in a way that no other memorial does. The memorial has unexpectedly compelled visitors to forge their own memory, to contribute their personal experiences to this place of collective memory. Almost since its dedication, visitors have left traces of their presence at the memorial in the form of medals, letters, photographs, beer cans, and even objects as unlikely as human ashes and a sliding glass door.

By 1991, as many as 30,000 "memories" of those who died in the Vietnam War had been left at the wall. Kristin Ann Hass, author of *Carried to the Wall: American Memory and the Vietnam Veterans Memorial*, noted:

> The Wall elicits a physical response. It has inspired visitors to represent their own grief, loss, rage, and despair. Contributing their private representations to public space, they cross a boundary between the private and the public, the nation and the citizen, powerfully claiming the memorial as their own.[34]

In a silent, profound act of communalization, people have chosen to leave something that represents the person lost and the bond shared between them at the memorial. This phenomenon that occurs at the Vietnam Veterans Memorial makes it clear that although the process of healing is as personal as the loss, it is dependent upon the reestablishment of a sense of community and a confirmation of the larger level of human connectedness.

Vietnam Veterans
Memorial

Most of the work contained in this volume of Pamphlet Architecture was completed before September 11, 2001, the day that the World Trade Centers collapsed after a terrorist attack. The scale of the violence and loss that occurred on that day is unprecedented. The case studies examined here point to how crucial the present is in terms of responding to what happened on that day. Both the MOVE conflict and the Buffalo Creek flood speak clearly to the fact that a trauma cannot be denied; it cannot be buried under new construction in hopes that it will eventually disappear. The concept of communalization, so crucial in recovery from PTSD, tells us that the traumatic experience must remain visible, that it must be shared. Transformation—the undoing of negative experiences through growth and insight—is an important lesson of the Great Chicago Fire, a lesson of spirit created out of trauma. The World Trade Center was an embodiment of history and dreams. Now it also represents the loss of thousands of lives. There is great potential in the reconstruction of the World Trade Center site, but only if it acknowledges everything that was once there and is now lost.

The Vietnam Veterans Memorial reminds us that trauma is individual; individual lives are lost, individual people are affected. The desire to respond, however, is communal. The recognition of September 11 as a loss of individuals was shared throughout Manhattan in the days that followed the bombing, as colored flyers of missing loved ones were posted throughout the city. With photographs, names, and descriptions of the missing individuals, the loss of 2,800 people, rather than lives, became very real. More than a search for missing loved ones, these spontaneous memorials were a subconscious communalization of individual grief, demonstrating an instinctive need for humans to respond. The significance of that moment must be remembered.

This proposal for the site of the MOVE bombing will remain theoretical. It is no longer possible to return to the time immediately after the bombing in Philadelphia and build an appropriate response to the traumatic events of the MOVE conflict. That opportunity has passed. But the opportunity to find an appropriate, thoughtful response to the events of September 11 is present. The loss of life is permanent. The bond between people and place can be reforged through deliberate, sensitive intervention.

Fragments of the World Trade Center

NOTES

1. "Final Report of the Philadelphia Special Investigation Commission," in Michael Boyette (with Randi Boyette), "Let It Burn": The Philadelphia Tragedy (Chicago: Contemporary Books, Inc., 1989), Appendix A, 281.

2. Boyette, 21.

3. Shaun D. Mullen, "May 1985, a bomb burned them out. Now the residents of Osage Avenue think it's time to move on," in The Philadelphia Inquirer, 12 May 2000.

4. American Psychiatric Association, Diagnostic and Statistical Manual of Mental Disorders, 3rd rev. ed. (Washington, D.C.: American Psychiatric Association, 1987), 247.

5. Allan Young, The Harmony of Illusions: Inventing Post-Traumatic Stress Disorder (Princeton: Princeton University Press, 1995), 7.

6. Young, 142.

7. Jonathan Shay, Achilles in Vietnam: Combat Trauma and the Undoing of Character (New York: Simon & Schuster, 1994), 4.

8. Shay, 181.

9. Robin Wagner-Pacifici, Discourse and Destruction: The City of Philadelphia Versus MOVE (Chicago: University of Chicago Press, 1994), 138.

10. One cop referred to having felt "left out" of Vietnam. Boyette, 160.

11. Kathleen Neal Cleaver, "Philadelphia Fire," in Transition 51 (May 1991): 156.

12. Young, 129.

13. John Africa, cited in Boyette, 39.

14. Boyette, 24.

15. MOVE, 25 Years on the MOVE (Self-published: May 1996), 19.

16. Shay, 23.

17. Quoted in Boyette, 143.

18. Ivan Illich, H_2O and the Waters of Forgetfulness (Dallas: The Dallas Institute of Humanities and Culture, 1985), 10.

19. MOVE, 32.

20. Illich, 18.

21. Quoted in Boyette, 145.

22. Wagner-Pacifici, 148.

23. Quoted in Kai T. Erikson, Everything in Its Path: Destruction of Community in the Buffalo Creek Flood (New York: Simon & Schuster, 1977), 46.

24. Erikson, 177.

25. Erikson, 150.

26. Erikson, 156.

27. S. M. Silver, J. P. Wilson, "Native American Healing and Purification Rituals for War Stress." In *Human Adaptation to Extreme Stress: From the Holocaust to Vietnam*, ed. John P. Wilson, Z. Harel, and B. Kahana (New York: Plenum Press, 1988), 10.

28. Elias Colbert and Everett Chamberlain, *Chicago and the Great Conflagration* (New York: Viking Press, 1971), 281.

29. The Eyewitnesses, www.chicagohs.org/fire/witnesses, 26 March 2002.

30. Donald L. Miller, *City of the Century: The Epic of Chicago and the Making of America* (New York: Simon & Schuster, 1997), 142.

31. Miller, 305.

32. Miller, 303.

33. "'At No Time in the History': John Wellborn Root," *Scribner's Magazine* 8 (October 1890), 416.

34. Kristin Ann Hass, *Carried to the Wall: American Memory and the Vietnam Veterans Memorial* (Berkeley: University of California Press, 1998), 21.

This pamphlet seeks to establish a psychological framework for generating architectural responses to traumatic events. Recovery from Post-Traumatic Stress Disorder (PTSD) relies on communalization and the construction of a narrative. In his 1994 book *Achilles in Vietnam: Combat Trauma and the Undoing of Character*, noted psychologist Jonathan Shay maintained that a narrative "can transform involuntary reexperiencing of traumatic events into memory of the events, thereby reestablishing authority over memory" (192). This concept of a narrative is temporal: an event takes place in time, with other events happening before, during, and after it. For the Cobbs Creek residents who were transformed by the MOVE conflict, the narrative is ongoing.

When this project was first conceived in January 2000, the rebuilt blocks on Osage Avenue and Pine Street were fully occupied; residents had been trying to move forward from the tragedy in these unsound homes for close to fifteen years. In preparation for its submission to the Pamphlet Architecture competition, and for its subsequent publication, the project was revisited between January and May 2002. During that time, another transformation was occurring, and continues to occur, in this small west Philadelphia community. The city is attempting to buy out residents in order to demolish the blocks. Clearly community is of vital importance to many residents, because at the time of this writing less than half have elected to move out. The city's plans for reconstruction (if drafted) are undisclosed. At the same time, New York City is struggling with how best to respond to another devastating trauma. The debate is ongoing over what is the "right way" to rebuild on the World Trade Center site. The reaction of this city to the events of September 11, 2001, point to the fact that there is rarely one clear way to respond to trauma.

The following pages present five architectural proposals for recovery on the site of the MOVE conflict. The first project is that of the author, conceived of and designed as a master's thesis project at the University of Pennsylvania. The four projects that follow are the products of a weekend-long charrette held in June 2002. The idea for a charrette was that of Kevin Lippert, publisher of Princeton Architectural Press, as a way of expanding the concepts developed in the foregoing essay by presenting multiple responses to the theory and to the MOVE conflict itself. Responses are constructed from the past and from the changing present of the site, as well as from the issues and beliefs that created the conflict. Each project is sited at a different point in time along the continuum of the conflict, suggesting its own narrative of the trauma and method for recovery.

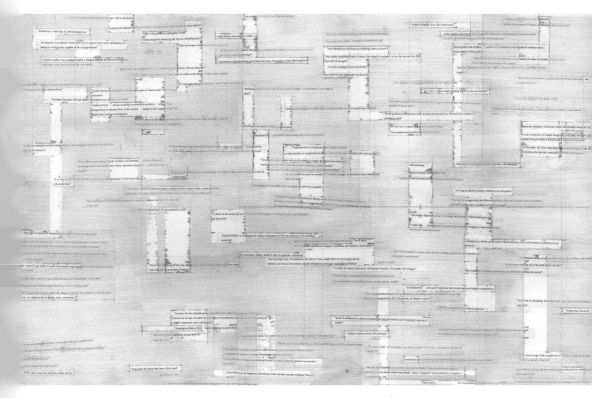

The MOVE conflict is first analyzed in collages generated from the theory of Robin Wagner-Pacifici, a sociologist who studies the impact of traumatic events on society. In her book *Discourse and Destruction: The City of Philadelphia Versus MOVE* (Chicago: University of Chicago Press, 1994), she interprets the MOVE conflict through the lens of discourse analysis, calling it "a strange hybrid, a charged space at the intersection of race, modernity, class, nature, urban life, and culture." It was a rigidity of beliefs, particularly those of MOVE, that drove the conflict to seemingly unresolvable extremes. Wagner-Pacifici maintains that no belief system is infallible, therefore a hybridization of discourse is essential. In this context, hybridization is "a practical acknowledgment of the incompleteness, the partiality of a given discursive formation," or, more literally, that "the same word will belong to two languages, two belief systems that intersect in a hybrid construction."

"Boundaries fluid at first…begin to harden around 1984."

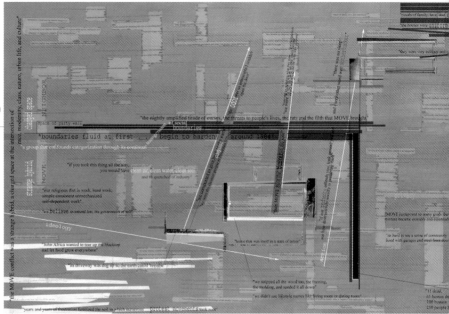

"Creation of imagery that maintains fidelity to the end, fidelity in the sense of remembering what the experience entailed and including its excrutiating truths in the self that is being recreated."

This hybridization theory is responded to in a sequence of three collages constructed from segments of writings that relate, either directly or indirectly, to the issues surrounding the MOVE conflict. The collages are a method of exploring the conflict as a social construction, both theoretically and spatially. In the first collage (left), the quotes are used to establish a horizontal linear system; new connections between seemingly dissident beliefs are drawn vertically. The second collage (right) seeks to pull the most crucial issues from the first collage and draw non-linear connections between them.

The final collage (following page) is a further reinterpretation of the spatial relationships created in the first two collages; quotes used are more in the language of resolution than conflict. Each collage seeks to create new imagery that retains the memory of that which preceded it.

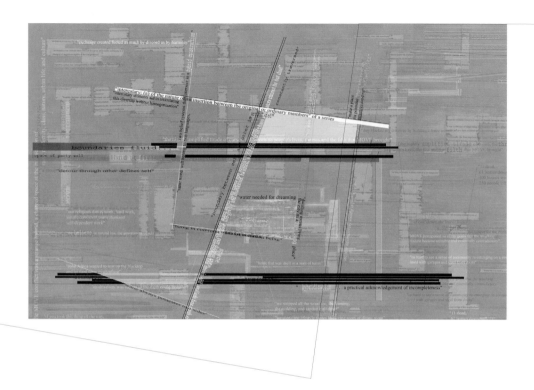

The rowhouse structure sets up a linear foundation on the site much in the way the quotes did in the first collage—a foundation that can be responded to nonlinearly. A study model translates these collage concepts into an architectural hybridization, showing possibilities for the intersection of different elements on the site.

For a hybrid architectural response to the MOVE conflict to be developed, its defining elements must be identified and analyzed. Five crucial "sites of exchange" from which the MOVE conflict was fought are identified: party wall, porch, backyard, bunker, and water. An architectural resolution of the conflict can be achieved through transformation and hybridization of these elements.

40

The hybridization theory is interpreted
three-dimensionally

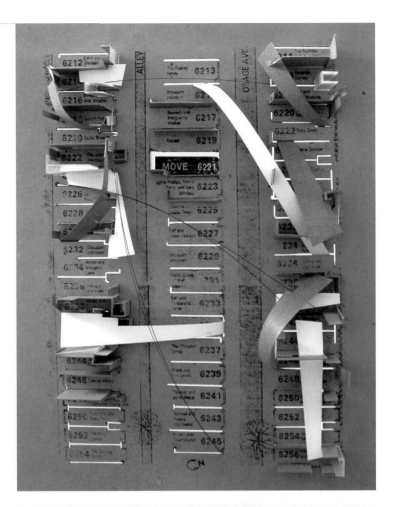

New opportunities for relationships
between elements are created

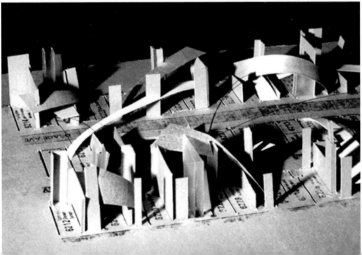

porch

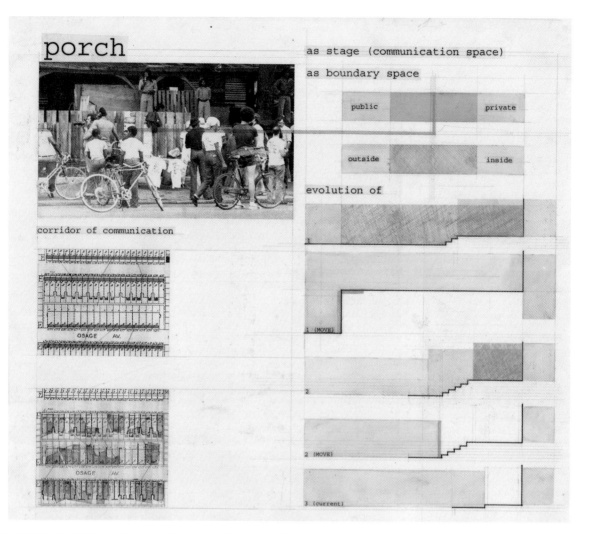

as stage (communication space)

as boundary space

| public | | private |

| outside | | inside |

evolution of

corridor of communication

1

1 (MOVE)

2

2 (MOVE)

3 (current)

OSAGE AV.

OSAGE AV.

The front porch underwent a dramatic transformation over the course of the MOVE conflict, from porch to stage to void. Today, the porch of the house as rebuilt has been all but eliminated; it is a small concrete slab closed in with a steel fence.

Any reconstruction must seek to undo this negative transformation and return the porch to its role of inhabitable boundary space and place of communication. In most urban contexts, the relationship between porches is linear, forming a corridor along the street. This reconstruction redefines the "front" by allowing this corridor to traverse the site, promoting new opportunities for communication between neighbors.

backyard

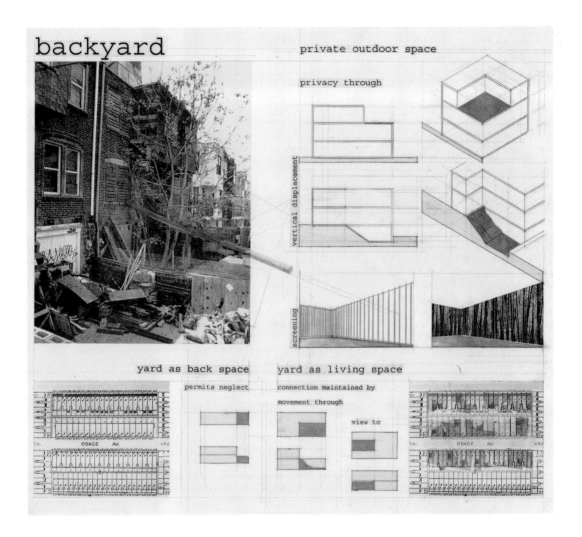

private outdoor space

privacy through

vertical displacement

screening

yard as back space

permits neglect

OSAGE AV.

yard as living space

connection maintained by

movement through

view to

OSAGE AV.

MOVE inhabited their backyard as if it were an extension of the interior space of the house. Rowhouse backyards, by nature of their limited access, are often neglected or abandoned spaces. In the reconstruction, the backyards can be located so that they have more intimate relationships to the houses' interiors. If an interior space wraps around or flanks the backyard, for example, the space becomes more occupiable.

A definitive aspect of the backyard is privacy. Privacy is often achieved in rowhouse backyards by walling them in. Here, alternative means of creating privacy, such as vertical displacement or screening, are considered.

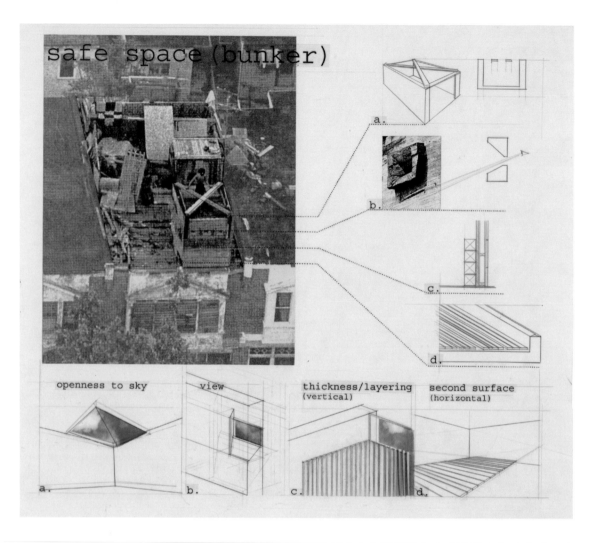

safe space (bunker)

openness to sky   view   thickness/layering (vertical)   second surface (horizontal)

a.   b.   c.   d.

The rooftop bunker, the most aggressive of MOVE's constructions, demands transformation. If the inherent violence of this construction can be briefly ignored, it becomes clear that MOVE was also trying to achieve security by moving up, above the space of the city. They sought to occupy the sky as they had the earth, through their use of the backyard. The bunker can be transformed into a positive construction, not of aggression but of healing.

The bunker was a small space, open to the sky, that provided views of the larger site; this can be reintroduced as a nonaggressive construction. MOVE built the bunker at a point when their traumatization reached a critical level, so it would be an appropriate transformation if this became a space that promoted reflection and recovery.

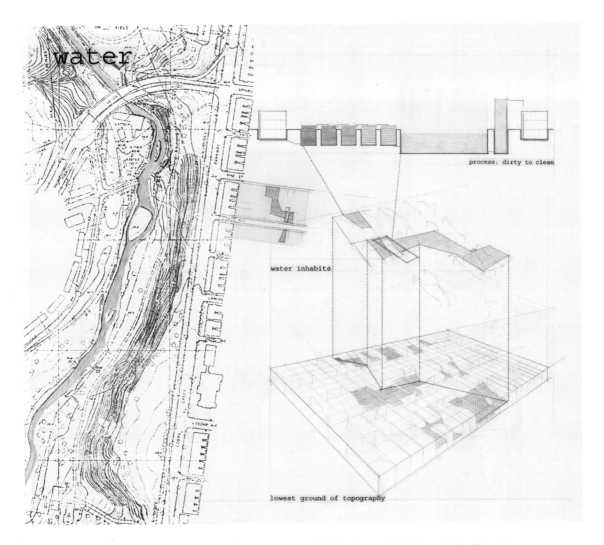

water

process: dirty to clean

water inhabits

lowest ground of topography

Although not architectural in nature, water is an element that can bring MOVE's original ideology into the reconstruction. Even though its persona became increasingly aggressive over the course of the conflict, MOVE's fundamental ideology was rooted in nonviolent ideas for a communal, natural urban existence. In every city water comes from a shared source—an embodiment of a communal existence.

Writer Ivan Illich maintained that water has the potential to have a profound effect on people, even if it has been piped through the city water supply system. In his 1985 book *H²O and the Waters of Forgetfulness*, he discussed the concept of building a new town lake in the city of Dallas, remarking that water is what is "needed for dreaming city as a dwelling space."

party wall

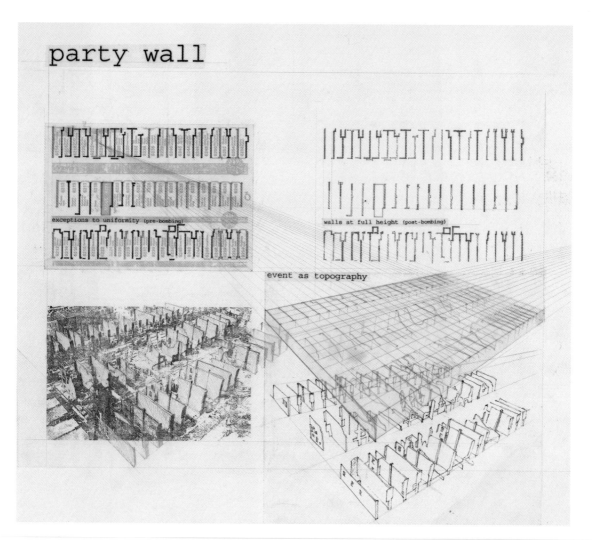

exceptions to uniformity (pre-bombing)

walls at full height (post-bombing)

event as topography

The party wall is a shared boundary on which each side relies for support. The walls, by nature, set up a basic linear structure on the site, as the quotes did in the earlier collages. In the site's prior construction, all architectural elements fit into this linear system. Introduction of nonlinear elements initiates hybridization. Penetration of the wall, without violation of privacy, starts to enable new relationships between the architectural elements and the residents themselves. If this boundary space can be occupied in a positive way, almost like a mutual transgression, it can begin to counteract some of the negative trespasses committed by MOVE on their neighbors. The most significant aspect of the party walls in the context of the MOVE conflict is that they were the only traces that remained of the site's occupancy before and immediately after the bombing. Although these walls no longer exist today, it is important to return to the bombing's aftermath, May 14, 1985, to find the proper response to this trauma.

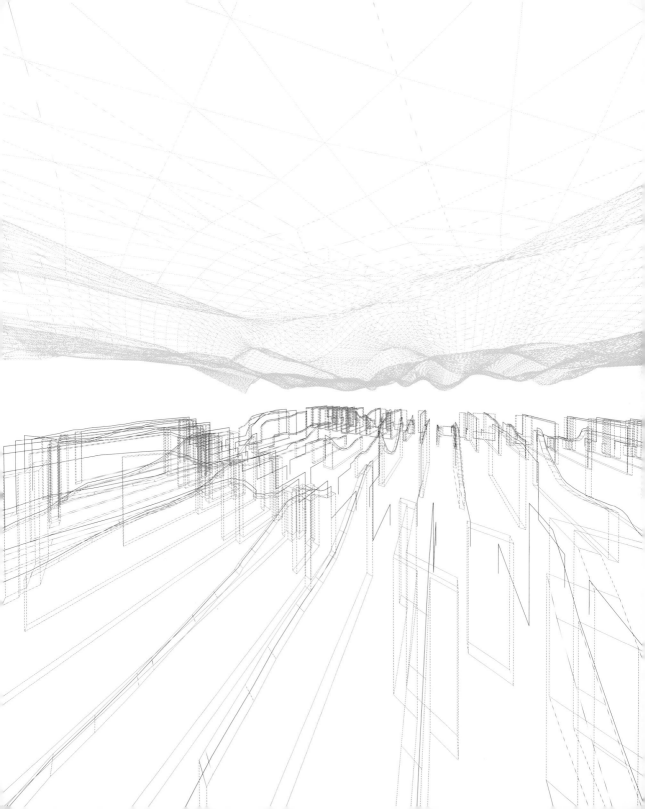

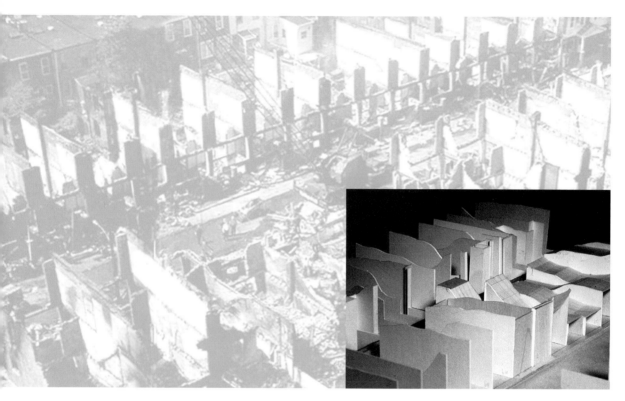

In *Trauma, Transformation, and Healing* (New York: Brunner/Mazel Inc., 1989), psychologist John Wilson maintained that recovery from PTSD occurs through the "creation of imagery that maintains fidelity to the end or to one's experience of inner deadness, fidelity in the sense of remembering what the experience entailed and including its excruciating truths in the self that is being recreated." After the fire, almost all of the party walls remained standing, but many of them were severely damaged, particularly those closest to the bomb's epicenter, the MOVE house at 6221 Osage Avenue.

It is in these damaged party walls that the potential for transformation is found. By leaving the party walls on the site in some form, they become the physical representation of the traumatic memory; an image of the past (and present) that starts to construct a narrative. From the pattern of damage to the walls a topography is created, an undulating surface with the deepest area occurring naturally at the place

Party walls, transformed

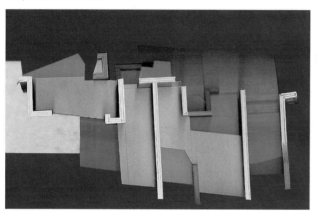 

where the bomb's impact was greatest. The damaged party walls are used in two ways. They act as the foundation upon which the new topography rests. They are also used in their original form; home-owners modified many of the walls over the years to have turns, jogs, and attachments. The walls as topography begin to establish sectional relationships; the walls as objects establish relationships in plan.

The basic form set up by the party walls as both objects and topography creates opportunities for new relationships between elements, such as front porch and backyard. The new topography on the site creates carved spaces, allowing outdoor spaces to become private simply from their differences in elevation.

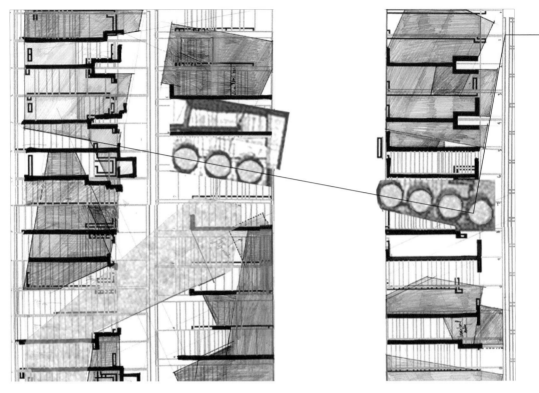

Water is reintroduced to the site first in the form of a reservoir—a large, calm place of reflection. Water is also used actively, in the form of a living machine. A living machine is a series of large tanks, fifteen feet in diameter, which cleans sewage water in a chemical-free environment by filtering it through plants and compost. Constructed inside a large greenhouse, it entails a seven-step process, each tank containing progressively cleaner water. The result is nonpotable but clean water. Each tank is filled with plants that create a gardenlike atmosphere while covering the sewage water and any accompanying smells. The living machine is placed in a shared open area of the site, a light-filled communal green space. The living machine embodies some of MOVE's ideologies, while emphasizing the idea of community and the possibility of finding a new way of dwelling in the city.

There are three primary elements of the site's reconstruction: housing, a living machine, and a memorial. Housing replaces the homes

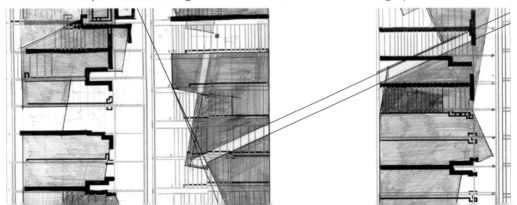

Living machine

that were lost. The living machine serves as an embodiment of MOVE's ideology, some aspects of which are sound and relevant to a modern urban existence. The memorial is a necessary acknowledgment of the lives that were lost on May 13, 1985. Like traumatization, recovery is a process that requires time. Maybe it is unreasonable to share MOVE's vision of a city returned to its natural state, but it is possible for architecture to have a positive, healthy relationship with both its inhabitants and its site. A sustainable architectural response to this conflict is drawn from issues raised by MOVE, but it also has a broader relevance.

Architecture can promote the process of recovery in a site, just as therapy and communalization promote the same in individuals, beyond the basic human need for sunlight and fresh air. Sustainable architecture seems to be the closest synthesis possible between the needs of people and place.

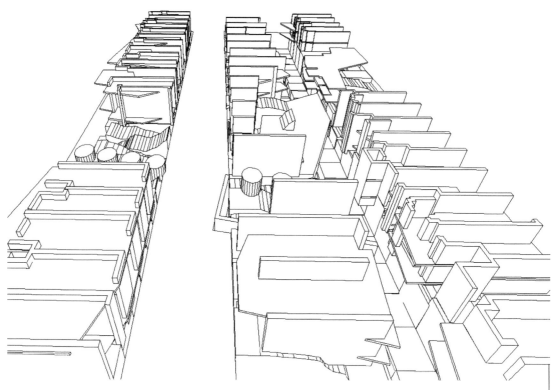

The tragic loss of life in the bombing is addressed in the form of a memorial that occupies the place where death occurred. The location of the MOVE house is the lowest point in the new topography; this is particularly appropriate because MOVE members sought to excavate and occupy the earth when they lived there. The memorial occupies the space where 6221 Osage Avenue once stood; it is the footprint of the rowhouse rotated off its original axis. The site's reservoir drops from sight below the living machine and reappears in approximately the same spot where MOVE's front porch had been, flowing down past the party wall and disappearing into the ground. A visitor enters at the "front porch" as well and follows the water down to the deepest point on the site; a place to sit is built at the base of the party wall. The memorial is simple: an excavated space, a place to sit, a party wall, and water.

Sketch of memorial

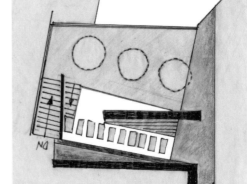

Prosthetic leg

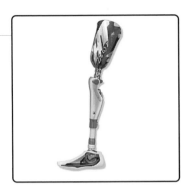

Prosthetic hands

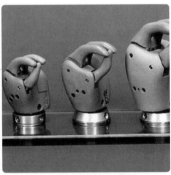

Scaffold

Jetway

Charcoal sketches for roof and stoop prostheses

A prosthetic bridges the gap between a physical trauma and the everyday. In medicine, this is not a formalist bridging but one of function and comfort for the traumatized. The prosthetic serves simultaneously as signifier of the trauma and its rehabilitation.

The current housing is an extension of the injury suffered in May 1985 at 6221 Osage Avenue. Razing the site again may solve problems caused by the hasty reconstruction, but it will not foster healing. The implementation of discrete architectural prostheses is intended to instigate a process of rehabilitation by returning stability and amenities lost in the site's reconstruction.

Current Osage Avenue streetscape

Collage: new insertions

Model: aerial view

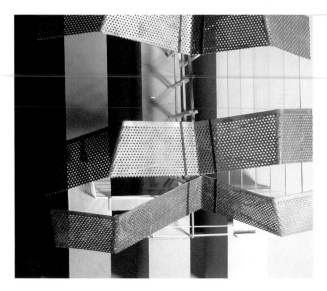

Details of section model

The shoddiness of current buildings perpetuates the loss of home. In encouraging abandonment, city policy further aggravates the loss.Rather than standing vacant, lots may serve as sites for prosthetic roof structures that would serve to protect and brace remaining dwellings and provide a framework for new construction.

A phantom MOVE house is a painful reminder of lives lost. Rather than fortified or guarded, this lot should be made transparent. The absence of a home on this site would both be a

profound acknowledgment of the deaths and provide access for future development (i.e. memorial, park, community space, "living machine") in the interior of the block.

These interventions address the original trauma and suggest future use. Their transformational capabilities begin a process of recovery that will continue until they are embedded within the built fabric (and memory) of the new community.

Section model: the prosthetic stoop at an existing rowhouse; the prosthetic roof structure at a demolished lot; access to the interior of the block at the empty MOVE lot

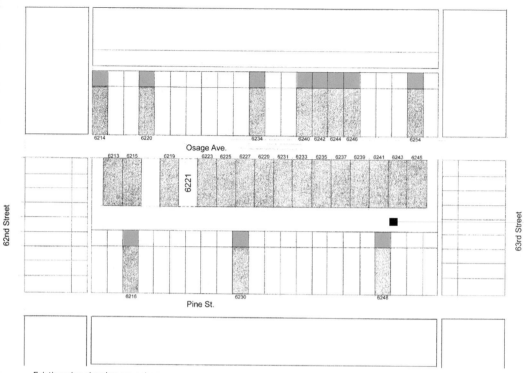

Osage Ave.

6214　6220　6234　6240 6242 6244 6246　6254

6213 6215　6219　6223 6225 6227 6229 6231 6233 6235 6237 6239 6241 6243 6245

6221

62nd Street

63rd Street

6216　6230　6248

Pine St.

Existing plan showing current occupancy

The city of Philadelphia has purchased and con-demned the majority of the MOVE neighborhood homes. The few residents who have paid their mortgages in full choose to remain. Our proposal removes the vacant homes and preserves the homes of those who elect to stay. Each remaining resident is provided additional private green space, and two small urban farms are introduced adjacent to an open market on the former MOVE address.

The reintroduction of private space restores the sense of community enjoyed by the residents prior to the MOVE tragedy. The land newly cleared of the now abandoned homes is therefore divided among the remaining residents, adding land adjacent to or near their property. On the north side of Osage, where yards were replaced with garages after 1985, each home is assigned a new parcel of land among those created along Pine Street.

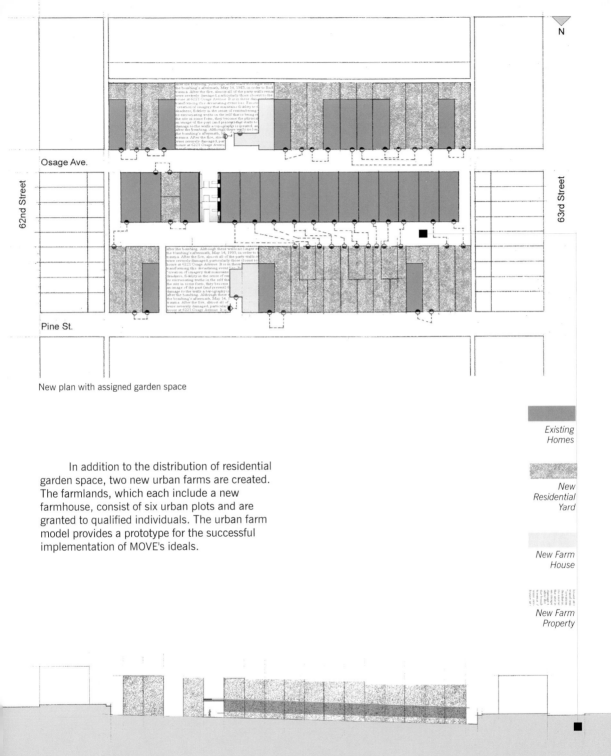

62nd Street

63rd Street

Osage Ave.

Pine St.

New plan with assigned garden space

Existing
Homes

New
Residential
Yard

New Farm
House

New Farm
Property

In addition to the distribution of residential garden space, two new urban farms are created. The farmlands, which each include a new farmhouse, consist of six urban plots and are granted to qualified individuals. The urban farm model provides a prototype for the successful implementation of MOVE's ideals.

The MOVE house at 6221 Osage has been occupied by the Philadelphia Police Department since its reconstruction. Because it is no longer necessary, a community market takes its place. Along the west wall, the market contains three built-in counters with seats for selling goods. Along the east wall is a continuous bench. Two of the selling areas are reserved for the farmers. Residents sell their own goods from the remaining counter.

When the market is not in session, the counters are folded into the bearing wall, creating a plaza. The market doors close at night to maintain the quiet nature of the neighborhood.

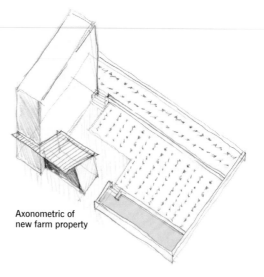

Axonometric of
new farm property

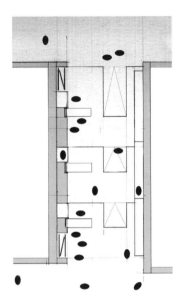
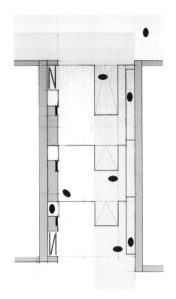
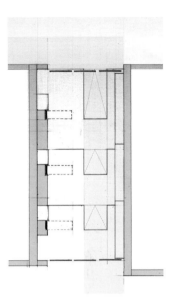

Marketplace (active on market days)   Plaza (community daytime gathering)   Night (folding panel doors close)

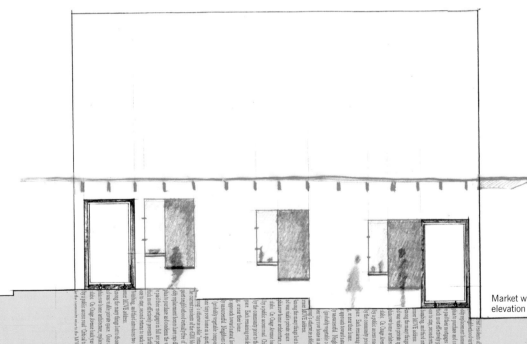

Market wall
elevation

View of market from alley

In speaking with a forty-two-year resident of Osage Avenue, it is apparent that a once close-knit social neighborhood has become isolated and detached by the MOVE conflict. The market encourages community interaction, whereas the plaza provides a place for individual reflection. The market site acknowledges the history embedded within it while promoting the growth and interaction of the current community.

The location of the new urban market on the MOVE property serves as a physical passage through the site, a community gathering place, and a memory device.

Although there are fewer permanent residents than there were previously, the new market draws people from the surrounding area. As the inhabited homes become vacant, the neighborhood continues to evolve. Residents may choose to create additional farms, keep the current homes, or rebuild anew.

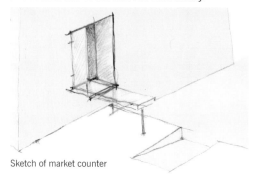

Sketch of market counter

View of market from Osage

Market niche detail

Bench detail

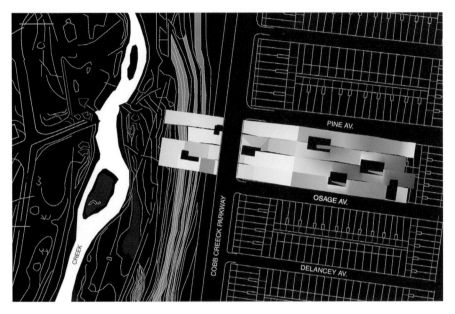

PARK

A terrible event can have a far-reaching impact. As Dickson shows, post-traumatic stress disorder can add a lingering infection to the initial blow. In this particular case, affliction has stolen substance from the place as well as the people surrounding the MOVE catastrophe. As architects it is our job to rehabilitate a sense of place where it has been lost. This does not mean rebuilding. In fact, a simple rebuilding has already done more harm than good, posing an (un)intentional ignorance of what has passed. The site—at least its

memory—is not the same. The response must address this. Gone is a sense of community. It is our duty to rehabilitate the area, acknowledge the tragedy (not surrender to it), and build.

John Africa's idea of letting nature take over is used in moderation. The park along Cobb's Creek is pulled under the parkway and into the neighborhood of Pine and Osage Avenue. As the park reaches the border of the old housing block, the landscape lifts off the ground and creates an inhabitable space underneath.

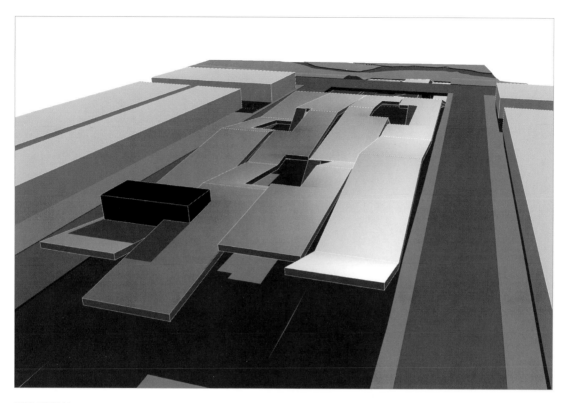

MEMORIAL

Four blackened steel walls are sited where the MOVE house once stood. The walls punch through the roof of the market. There are no windows or doors in the box. Hung from the roof, the walls don't quite reach the ground. Light seeps out from the bottom of this roofless structure. There is nothing of the events of May 13, 1985, written at the memorial. It is an empty box whose memory would be explained by those familiar and unfamiliar with the tragedy. The exact details, which no plaque could explain without bias, would eventually ebb and flow, lending to the creation of a story for this place. It would become both a history and a myth, written by word of mouth.

MARKET

Under the earthen canopy is an open-air market. Similar to Center City's Reading Terminal Market and south Philadelphia's Italian Market, individual entrepreneurs will have their own stands where they can sell sundry wares. People can enjoy the bounty of the market on the rooftop leading down to the creek.

Holes punched in the canopy provide
vertical circulation and allow light to filter into the
market below. One can picnic on the roof or, if
athletically inclined, run along it. The faceted
landscape's rhythm is influenced by the spacing
of partitions of the former block.

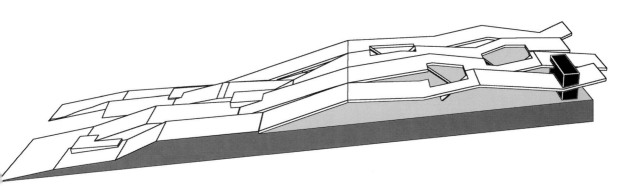

71

Our proposal initiates a process of healing and redevelopment on Osage Avenue through sequential phases that trigger community interaction. By focusing on the treatment stages for Post-Traumatic Stress Disorder, the proposed sequence addresses the memory of the event and the collective trauma experienced and suggests opportunities for regeneration.

The redevelopment of Osage Avenue creates new community gathering platforms to encourage dialogue and interaction, and new housing units to activate the evolution of each lot. The DPTNP framework is meant to prepare the site for changes, which will eventually grow beyond the prescribed sequence to assume their own cycle of transformation.

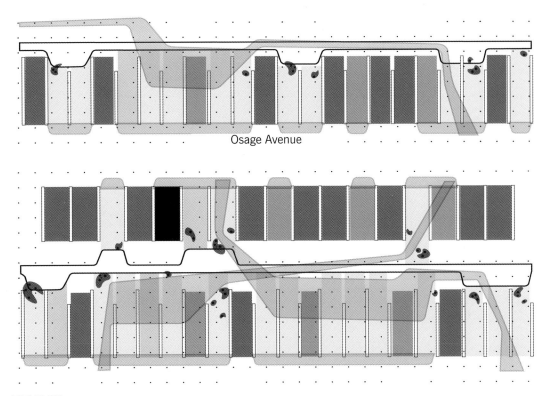

Osage Avenue

MEMORY

DIALOGUE

HABITATION

73

MEMORY

The trauma experienced by the MOVE group and the community is the starting point of this proposal. Through the removal of the vacant rowhouses—thirty-nine in total today—a new landscape of partition walls emerges reminiscent of the trace of the fire, which destroyed this community. The lot of the MOVE house is filled with a solid monolith remembering the eleven lives lost on the site. The impact of the monolith, the size of a rowhouse, will slowly diminish as new houses are built around it.

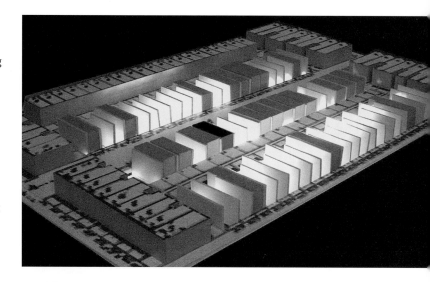

SEQUENTIAL PHASES

Dynamic Post-Trauma Neighborhood Planning is a framework based on time and flexibility. This framework evolves in phases that allow for multiple transformations at various stages of the healing process of the community. The rate of transformation depends on the community, the individuals who live in it, and their changing needs. Thus, if tenants do not wish to leave their houses, the new development will gradually emerge around them at different intervals.

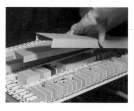

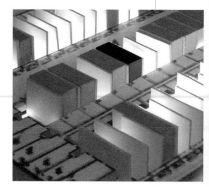

REMOVE
the derelict unoccupied rowhouses, leaving a landscape of illuminated partition walls.

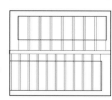

INSERT
a black monolith at 6221 Osage Avenue in remembrance of the eleven MOVE members who died.

2002 generational time line - 25 years

DIALOGUE

New areas for gathering are prescribed to bring the community together, in an attempt to heal through various modes of interaction. The community gardens, the front stoops (here acting as raised stages much like the front porch), and the elevated platforms (surfaces that enable various activities) are spaces where these modes can start to take shape.

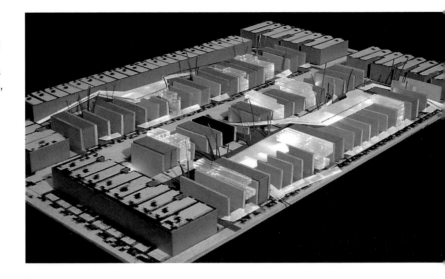

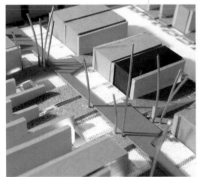
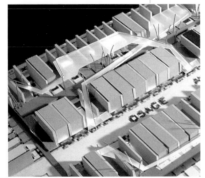

PLACE
gardens in the cavities for remediation of the soil and create new alleyways and parking bays.

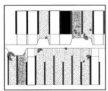

CONSTRUCT
elevated community platforms, utilizing the partition walls as a structural element.

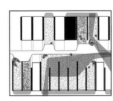

INHABIT
Osage Avenue with new homes built around the stoops and platforms.

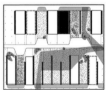

2027

HABITATION

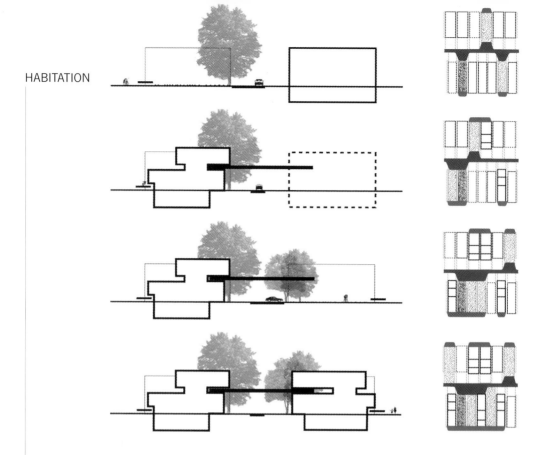

Habitation is not only the individual housing unit but also the gradual transformation and growth of the community. The proposal prescribes an incremental rehabitation. A generation might pass from the time of the removal of the abandoned houses, through the transition period of the gardens, to the construction of platforms and the new houses.

The new rowhouse has been built around the stoop and platform and assumes a new relationship with the community through these two public elements. As phases progress, other undetermined relationships form between the public and the private spaces.

COMMUNITY PROGRAMS

Community gardens

Produce market

Leisure and recreation

COMPONENTS

MEMORY
PARTITION
WALLS

MOVE
MEMORIAL
MONOLITH

ALLEYWAY
AND PARKING
BAYS

TRANSITION
GARDENS

TREE CLUSTERS

FRONT STOOPS

EVENT PLATFORM

ROWHOUSES

NEW OCCUPIED REMOVED

POINT-GRID
LIGHTS

Neighborhood celebration

Festivities and entertainment

Picnics

ABOUT THE AUTHOR

Johanna Saleh Dickson began researching the MOVE conflict as a Masters candidate at the University of Pennsylvania School of Architecture in Philadelphia, the city in which that conflict took place. Having studied psychology as an undergraduate, she approached the problem of rebuilding on the site through a framework that enlisted architecture in the task of emotional recovery. After receiving her degree, Dickson moved to New York City, where she practices architecture in the firm of Kostow Greenwood Architects. The Pamphlet Architecture competition held in the Fall of 2001, coupled with the tragic events of September 11, provided ample incentive for her to revisit her work and extend her investigation of the impact of traumatic events upon the build environment and its inhabitants.

CONTRIBUTORS

Mark Gardner currently practices architecture in New York City. His interests center on the relationship between art and architecture and the role of memory and place. He holds a Bachelor degree in architecture from Georgia Tech and a Master of Architecture from the University of Pennsylvania.

Todd Hoehn is currently an architect at Weiss/Manfredi Architects and is co-founder of THinKT lab, a venture that explores speculative projects in landscape and architecture. He earned a Master of Architecture from the University of Pennsylvania. He also studied at the Architectural Association in London and received a Bachelor in Industrial Design from the Milwaukee Institute of Art and Design.

Henry Hsu currently resides in New York City. Presently working in public relations for the fashion industry, his interests focus on architecture, design, and their relationship to culture. He holds a Bachelor degree in Anthropology from Grinnell College and a Master of Architecture from the University of Pennsylvania.

Thomas Kirchner earned his Master of Architecture from the University of Pennsylvania and Bachelor degree in philosophy from Colgate University. He recently coauthored a master plan for the Venetian Arsenale, which was published in Fondamenta Nuovissime by the International Laboratory of Architecture and Urban Design. He currently practices architecture in Philadelphia.

Richard McNamara was raised in Lancaster, Pennsylvania. He studied economics at Wesleyan University and obtained his Master of Architecture from the University of Pennsylvania. He currently works at SPF:a in Culver City, California.

Gaetane Michaux hails from Brussels. After studying sculpture, she earned her degree in architecture from the Victor Horta Institute for Architecture. She moved to New York City three years ago, where she works for Kohn Pedersen Fox Associates. In addition to architecture, her interests include photography and graphic design. Her work can be seen in Neomu.

Alexandra Schmidt-Ullrich received a Master in Architecture from the University of Pennsylvania, where she currently teaches undergraduate architecture and works in the Graduate School of Fine Arts Fabrication Laboratory. She resides in Philadelphia and practices at a local architecture firm. Her interests range from photography and printmaking to industrial and furniture design with a strong emphasis on material quality and craftsmanship.

Edowa Shimizu was born and raised in Tokyo. He attended Vassar College and the Architectural Association in London, and received his Master of Architecture from the University of Pennsylvania, where he frequently returns as a guest critic. After working in several architectural firms, he cofounded an event planning and production company in New York City and can often be found moonlighting as a dj.

Brian Slocum earned his Bachelor degree in architecture from Georgia Tech and Master of Architecture from Columbia University. He currently practices in New York City and also conducts independent research on the roles of experimentation and time in the processes of design, construction, inhabitation, and renovation.

Karen Tamir, a landscape architect, currently works at Field Operations. She earned her Master of Landscape Architecture from the University of Pennsylvania. She is a member of the Summer Institute program's teaching faculty and is also co-founder of THinKT lab, a collaborative venture involving landscape and architecture.

Chris Warren is originally from Denver. He first studied architecture at the University of Colorado at Boulder and obtained his Master of Architecture from the University of Pennsylvania. He currently works at Morphosis Architects in Santa Monica.

ACKNOWLEDGMENTS

I would like to thank my family and friends for their patience and support while I worked on this book. William Braham, Associate Professor of Architecture at the University of Pennsylvania and my thesis advisor, helped me develop a project out of an initial concept. Mark Gardner first encouraged me to enter the Pamphlet Architecture competition. Ted Schenkelberg and my aunt, Deborah Dickson, gave me valuable suggestions for the text. My editor, Nancy Eklund Later, gave me the support and clarity I needed to turn this thesis into a book. I am very grateful to my friends, who expanded my work through their contributions of strong ideas and thoughtful designs. I would especially like to thank my father, who quietly drew me toward architecture, and my sister, who is supportive of me in every way. I dedicate this book to my mother.

—Johanna Saleh Dickson

CREDITS

The author would like to acknowledge the use of the following images in this pamphlet: Michael Boyette (with Randi Boyette), *"Let It Burn": The Philadelphia Tragedy* (Chicago: Contemporary Books, Inc., 1989), pages xi, 24; Chicago Historical Society, Web site, www.chicagohs.org/fire/fanning/pic0293.html, 26 March 2002, page 29; Johanna Saleh Dickson, page 8; FMC Technologies, Inc., Glass Passenger Boarding Bridge (© 1998), Web site, www.jetway.com, page 54 (bottom); Public Broadcasting System, Web site, www.pbs.org/art21/artists/lin/card1.html, 3 April 2002, page 30; James Natchwey, *Time* (September 11, 2001), 24-25, page 29; *National Geographic*, pages 76 (bottom left), 76 (bottom center), 77 (bottom left); National Park Service, in Mary Malone, *Maya Lin: Architect and Artist* (Sprinfield, N.J.: Enslow Publishers, 1995), page 31; Otto Bock Health Care, 3C100 C-Leg System, Web site, www.ottobockus.com, page 54 (top); *Philadelphia Bulletin*/Temple University Photojournalism Collection, in Michael Boyette (with Randi Boyette), *"Let It Burn": The Philadelphia Tragedy* (Chicago: Contemporary Books, Inc., 1989), pages 6, 9, 15, 16, 18; *The Philadelphia Daily News*, 27 April 1978, page 17; *The Philadelphia Inquirer* (March 1984–January 1986), pages 19 (bottom), 22, 25; Phillip Morris advertising campaign, page 76 (bottom right); Alexandra Schmidt-Ullrich, pages 64 (background), 65 (background); Edowa Shimizu, page 77 (bottom right); Brian Slocum, page 54 (lower middle); Brittain Stone, page 77 (bottom center) United States Geological Survey, Web site, http://ngmsvr.wr.usgs.gov/ngmdb/ngm_catalog.html. March, 2000, page 19 (top); Variety Ability Systems, Inc., VASI hands (© 2001), Web site, www.vasi.on.ca, page 54 (upper middle); West Virginia Division of Culture and History, Web site, www.wvculture.org/history/buffcreek/bctitle.html, 19 March 2002, page 27.

CREDITS FOR QUOTED MATERIAL

page 4	Michael Boyette, *"Let It Burn": The Philadelphia Tragedy"* (Chicago: Contemporary Books, Inc., 1989), 21.
page 8	John Africa in MOVE, *25 Years on the MOVE* (Self-published: May 1996), 22.
page 11	John P. Wilson, *Trauma, Transformation, and Healing: An Integrative Approach to Theory Research and Post-Traumatic Therapy* (New York: Brunner/Mazel, Inc., 1989), 41.
page 12	MOVE, in *25 Years on the MOVE*, 68.
page 13	Sharon Sims Cox (as told to Carol Saline), "My Life in MOVE: One Woman Reveals what it was really like," in *Philadelphia Magazine* (September 1985), 170.
pages 14, 21 (bottom), 22	MOVE member, culled from articles that appeared in *The Philadelphia Inquirer* (March 1984–January 1986).
page 15	Robin Wagner-Pacifici, *Discourse and Destruction: The City of Philadelphia Versus MOVE* (Chicago: University of Chicago Press, 1994), 27.
page 21 (top)	Louise James, cited in Wagner-Pacifici, 39.